D0468465

LIVING WITH DISEASES AND DISORDERS

Crohn's Disease and Other Digestive Disorders

LIVING WITH DISEASES AND DISORDERS

ADHD and Other Behavior Disorders

Allergies and Other Immune System Disorders

Asthma, Cystic Fibrosis, and Other Respiratory Disorders

Autism and Other Developmental Disorders

Cancer and Sickle Cell Disease

Cerebral Palsy and Other Traumatic Brain Injuries

Crohn's Disease and Other Digestive Disorders

Depression, Anxiety, and Bipolar Disorders

Diabetes and Other Endocrine Disorders

Migraines and Seizures

Muscular Dystrophy and Other Neuromuscular Disorders

LIVING WITH DISEASES AND DISORDERS

Crohn's Disease and Other Digestive Disorders

REBECCA SHERMAN

SERIES ADVISOR
HEATHER L. PELLETIER, Ph.D.
Pediatric Psychologist, Hasbro Children's Hospital
Clinical Assistant Professor, Warren Alpert Medical School of Brown University

MASON CREST

Mason Crest
450 Parkway Drive, Suite D
Broomall, PA 19008
www.masoncrest.com

© 2018 by Mason Crest, an imprint of National Highlights, Inc. All rights reserved. No part of this publication may be reproduced or transmitted in any form or by any means, electronic or mechanical, including photocopying, recording, taping, or any information storage and retrieval system, without permission from the publisher.

MTM Publishing, Inc.
435 West 23rd Street, #8C
New York, NY 10011
www.mtmpublishing.com

President: Valerie Tomaselli
Vice President, Book Development: Hilary Poole
Designer: Annemarie Redmond
Copyeditor: Peter Jaskowiak
Editorial Assistant: Leigh Eron

Series ISBN: 978-1-4222-3747-2
Hardback ISBN: 978-1-4222-3754-0
E-Book ISBN: 978-1-4222-8035-5

Library of Congress Cataloging-in-Publication Data
Names: Sherman, Rebecca, author.
Title: Crohn's disease and other digestive disorders / by Rebecca Sherman; series consultant: Heather Pelletier, PhD, Hasbro Children's Hospital, Alpert Medical School/Brown University.
Description: Broomall, PA: Mason Crest, [2018] | Series: Living with diseases and disorders | Includes index. | Audience: Age: 12+ | Audience: Grade 7 to 8.
Identifiers: LCCN 2016053133 (print) | LCCN 2016053886 (ebook) | ISBN 9781422237540 (hardback : alk. paper) | ISBN 9781422280355 (ebook)
Subjects: LCSH: Crohn's disease—Juvenile literature. | Digestive organs—Diseases—Juvenile literature. | Digestive organs—Diseases—Treatment—Juvenile literature.
Classification: LCC RC862.E52 S54 2018 (print) | LCC RC862.E52 (ebook) | DDC 616.3/44—dc23
LC record available at https://lccn.loc.gov/2016053133

Printed and bound in the United States of America.

First printing
9 8 7 6 5 4 3 2 1

QR CODES AND LINKS TO THIRD PARTY CONTENT

You may gain access to certain third party content ("Third Party Sites") by scanning and using the QR Codes that appear in this publication (the "QR Codes"). We do not operate or control in any respect any information, products or services on such Third Party Sites linked to by us via the QR Codes included in this publication and we assume no responsibility for any materials you may access using the QR Codes. Your use of the QR Codes may be subject to terms, limitations, or restrictions set forth in the applicable terms of use or otherwise established by the owners of the Third Party Sites. Our linking to such Third Party Sites via the QR Codes does not imply an endorsement or sponsorship of such Third Party Sites, or the information, products or services offered on or through the Third Party Sites, nor does it imply an endorsement or sponsorship of this publication by the owners of such Third Party Sites.

TABLE OF CONTENTS

Key Icons to Look for:

 Words to Understand: These words with their easy-to-understand definitions will increase the reader's understanding of the text, while building vocabulary skills.

 Sidebars: This boxed material within the main text allows readers to build knowledge, gain insights, explore possibilities, and broaden their perspectives by weaving together additional information to provide realistic and holistic perspectives.

 Educational Videos: Readers can view videos by scanning our QR codes, which will provide them with additional educational content to supplement the text. Examples include news coverage, moments in history, speeches, iconic sports moments, and much more.

 Text-Dependent Questions: These questions send the reader back to the text for more careful attention to the evidence presented there.

 Research Projects: Readers are pointed toward areas of further inquiry connected to each chapter. Suggestions are provided for projects that encourage deeper research and analysis.

 Series Glossary of Key Terms: This back-of-the-book glossary contains terminology used throughout the series. Words found here increase the reader's ability to read and comprehend higher-level books and articles in this field.

SERIES INTRODUCTION

According to the Chronic Disease Center at the Centers for Disease Control and Prevention, over 100 million Americans suffer from a chronic illness or medical condition. In other words, they have a health problem that lasts three months or more, affects their ability to perform normal activities, and requires frequent medical care and/or hospitalizations. Epidemiological studies suggest that between 15 and 18 million of those with chronic illness or medical conditions are children and adolescents. That's roughly one out of every four children in the United States.

These young people must exert more time and energy to complete the tasks their peers do with minimal thought. For example, kids with Crohn's disease, ulcerative colitis, or other digestive issues have to plan meals and snacks carefully, to make sure they are not eating food that could irritate their stomachs or cause pain and discomfort. People with cerebral palsy, muscular dystrophy, or other physical limitations associated with a medical condition may need help getting dressed, using the bathroom, or joining an activity in gym class. Those with cystic fibrosis, asthma, or epilepsy may have to avoid certain activities or environments altogether. ADHD and other behavior disorders require the individual to work harder to sustain the level of attention and focus necessary to keep up in school.

Living with a chronic illness or medical condition is not easy. Identifying a diagnosis and adjusting to the initial shock is only the beginning of a long journey. Medications, follow-up appointments and procedures, missed school or work, adjusting to treatment regimens, coping with uncertainty, and readjusting expectations are all hurdles one has to overcome in learning how to live one's best life. Naturally, feelings of sadness or anxiety may set in while learning how to make it all work. This is especially true for young people, who may reach a point in their medical journey when they have to rethink some of their original goals and life plans to better match their health reality.

Chances are, you know people who live this reality on a regular basis. It is important to remember that those affected by chronic illness are family members, neighbors, friends, or maybe even our own doctors. They are likely navigating the demands of the day a little differently, as they balance the specific accommodations necessary to manage their illness. But they have the same desire to be productive and included as those who are fortunate not to have a chronic illness.

This set provides valuable information about the most common childhood chronic illnesses, in language that is engaging and easy for students to grasp. Each chapter highlights important vocabulary words and offers text-dependent questions to help assess comprehension. Meanwhile, educational videos (available by scanning QR codes) and research projects help connect the text to the outside world.

Our mission with this set is twofold. First, the volumes provide a go-to source for information about chronic illness for young people who are living with particular conditions. Each volume in this set strives to provide reliable medical information and practical advice for living day-to-day with various challenges. Second, we hope these volumes will also help kids without chronic illness better understand and appreciate how people with health challenges live. After all, if one in four young people is managing a health condition, it's safe to assume that the majority of our youth already know someone with a chronic illness, whether they realize it or not.

With the growing presence of social media, bullying is easier than ever before. It's vital that young people take a moment to stop and think about how they are more similar to kids with health challenges than they are different. Poor understanding and low tolerance for individual differences are often the platforms for bullying and noninclusive behavior, both in person and online. Living with Diseases and Disorders strives to close the gap of misunderstanding.

The ultimate solution to the bullying problem is surely an increase in empathy. We hope these books will help readers better understand and appreciate not only the daily struggles of people living with chronic conditions, but their triumphs as well.

—Heather Pelletier, Ph.D.
Hasbro Children's Hospital
Warren Alpert Medical School of Brown University

WORDS TO UNDERSTAND

absorb: a chemical or physical process of taking one substance into another.

calorie: a measure of energy in food.

carbohydrates: molecules from which animals derive energy; includes sugars, starches, and cellulose.

gastrointestinal (GI) tract: a series of linked organs that form a long tube from the mouth to the anus; also called the digestive tract.

ingest: to bring a substance into the body.

nutrients: substances in food that provide the essential materials to support life and growth.

peristalsis: a wave-like movement created when muscles of the intestines continually contract and relax.

proteins: complex molecules made from long chains of smaller molecules called amino acids; used to build and repair cells in the body, and for energy.

sphincter: a ring-like muscle at the opening of a hollow organ that tightens or relaxes to close or open the hole.

CHAPTER ONE

What Is the Digestive System?

I f you or someone you love has a digestive disease or disorder, such as Crohn's disease, ulcerative colitis, celiac disease, or irritable bowel syndrome (IBS), you probably have a lot of questions about what is happening to your or that person's body. Before you can understand how disease affects you, it helps to understand how your body works. In this chapter, you'll learn about how the digestive system functions.

Your Body Needs Energy

Energy. Your body needs it for everything you do: running, talking, even turning the pages of this book. You also need energy to take care of automatic bodily processes. These are necessary activities your body conducts unconsciously—that is, without thinking about it. Energy is the foundation of all basic life processes. Your cells need energy just to survive. During

Digestive problems are very common. As many as 70 million Americans have some type of digestive disorder.

childhood and adolescence, the human body needs extra energy to power growth and development.

Animals get energy when they **ingest** and **absorb** food through a process you know well: eating. But to get that energy, your body must break down the food you eat into its molecular parts: fats, **proteins**, and **carbohydrates**. These molecules are then broken down even further, into smaller molecules like fatty acids, amino acids, and simple sugars. These smaller molecules can be transported through cell walls for use by cells all over the body.

A set of hollow organs ingests your food, breaks it down into its molecular components, absorbs the energy and **nutrients** those components contain, and eliminates waste products once the process is complete. These hollow organs form a continuous, fantastically twisting tube that traverses your body from your mouth to your bottom. Collectively, they are known as the **gastrointestinal tract**, or the GI tract.

The GI Tract

The GI tract begins with the mouth, where food and drink first enter the body. The mouth is responsible for chewing food into smaller bits that will fit through the next stage of the GI tract, the esophagus. The mouth produces saliva, a digestive juice that helps to ease the passage of food down the esophagus. Saliva also breaks down a form of carbohydrate known as starch.

The esophagus, the tube leading from the mouth to the stomach, transports chewed-up food via a muscular movement known as swallowing. At its lower end, a ring-like muscle called a **sphincter** relaxes to allow the passage of food into the stomach. If this lower esophageal sphincter misfires or has trouble functioning, a person may suffer from a condition known as reflux—which is when the contents of the stomach travel the wrong way back up the esophagus.

THE MANY VARIETIES OF POOP

Feces. Stool. Excrement. These are all more formal words for what remains after the digestive system has finished with your food—poop, in other words. It might be impolite to talk about stool, but it is perfectly normal to notice what your stool looks like. A recent French study found that more than 50 percent of study participants "inspected their feces" in the toilet at least half of the time they used the bathroom!

For doctors trying to diagnose or treat digestive diseases and disorders, a person's stool provides valuable information. Doctors may ask for a stool sample. They may ask about frequency, or how often you poop. They may also ask about the consistency of stools—whether your poop is hard or soft, solid or liquid, in large or small pieces.

In 1997 researchers developed the Bristol Stool Chart to help patients and doctors categorize their poop on a scale from 1 to 7. Stools on the lower end of the scale have generally taken longer to pass through the gut. They are associated with constipation. Those on the higher end have traveled more quickly, leaving the body before the colon has had time to absorb liquid. They are associated with diarrhea. A too-rapid transit of food through the gut can be a sign of inflammation in the small or large intestines.

In the stomach, the real work of digestion begins. The walls of the stomach secrete a digestive juice called gastric acid, which breaks down chewed-up food particles at the molecular level. Gastric acid is particularly good at breaking down proteins. The muscles of the stomach mix the food particles and the gastric acid together into a semi-liquid mash called chyme. Chyme is stored by the lower stomach and released a little bit at a time through another sphincter—the pyloric sphincter—into the next part of the GI tract: the small intestine.

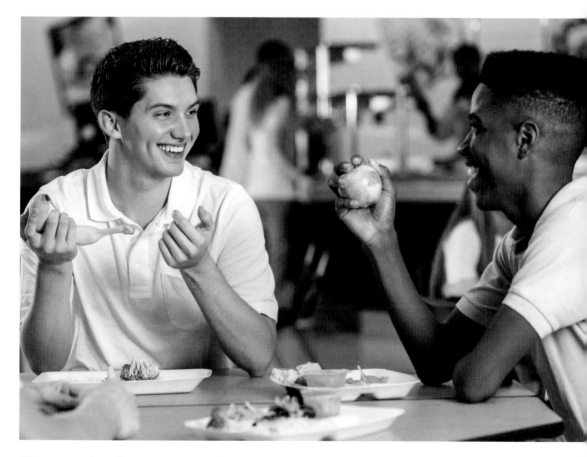

Chewing and swallowing is just the first step in a complex process through which your body gathers nutrients out of what you eat.

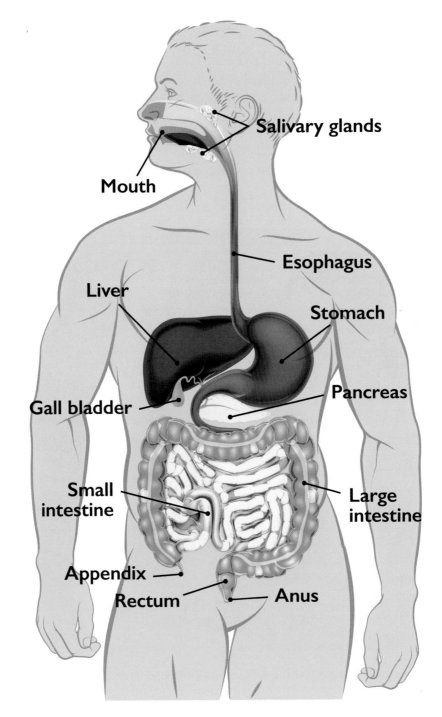

The human digestive system.

The small intestine breaks food molecules into ever-smaller molecules, using the gastric juices released into the small intestine from the stomach, digestive juices from the pancreas, and some digestive juice produced by the small intestine itself. Bile from the liver and gallbladder enter the small intestine through ducts to help break down fats. Once broken down, these smaller molecules are absorbed through the walls of the small intestine into the bloodstream or the lymphatic system (which carries white blood cells) for transport around the body for use.

The small intestine requires a lot of space to digest and absorb chyme. In an adult, the tube of the small intestine measures about 1 inch in diameter—but it is between 10 and 20 feet in length! To fit all that length into your belly, the small intestine curves and folds upon itself many times. In order to move digested food particles down this long folding tube, the muscles of the small intestine contract and relax in a wave-like action called **peristalsis**.

The small intestine has three regions: the duodenum, the jejunum, and the ileum. The duodenum is where the contents of the stomach and the digestive juices from the small intestine, liver, and pancreas mix. The partially digested food then travels to the jejunum, where most of the absorption of food molecules takes place. The third and longest region is the ileum, where any remaining nutrients in the digested food should be absorbed. By the end of food's journey through the small intestine, only waste products remain, called fecal matter. These are transferred onto the next stage of the GI tract, the large intestine.

EDUCATIONAL VIDEO

Scan this QR code for a video about the workings of the digestive system.

The large intestine is a tube about 2.5 inches in diameter, more than twice the diameter of the small intestine. It is much shorter than the small intestine, however. It has two main parts: the colon and the rectum. The colon's job is to absorb water from fecal matter as that matter is moved along on its journey out of the body. When the colon is working properly, feces—otherwise known as poop—should leave the body in a solid form. The colon also hosts great numbers of bacteria. The first region of the colon, called the cecum, is a pouch-shaped structure attached to the appendix. Fecal matter is mixed with bacteria in the cecum before being moved on for a journey that takes it up, across, and down the abdominal cavity through sections of the colon named for the directions they travel. After one final s-shaped curve, known as the sigmoid colon, feces are delivered to the final segment of the large intestine, called the rectum. They are stored here until a person uses the bathroom. The feces then leave the body through the anus. (Don't forget to flush!)

The Long History of Digestive Complaint and Disease

When the GI tract is functioning well, it's easy to take pleasure in eating and drinking. But when something goes wrong with any one of the GI tract's parts, eating and pooping can become a source of anxiety and pain. Diseases and disorders in any section of the GI tract can result in very serious health issues, as well as difficulties in managing daily life. People have suffered from problems of the digestive system for all of recorded history. The word *diarrhea*, for frequent and fluid stools, comes from an ancient Greek word meaning "flow through." It appears in the earliest medical texts dating back to Greece in the fifth century BCE. From the ancient Greeks we also get the root of the word *hemorrhoids*, for swollen or bleeding veins around the anus generally caused by irritation from trying to pass very hard, dry stool. A Hindu medical text from sixth-century India describes the symptoms of "an abnormal increase in the production of fecal matter," as well as those of the

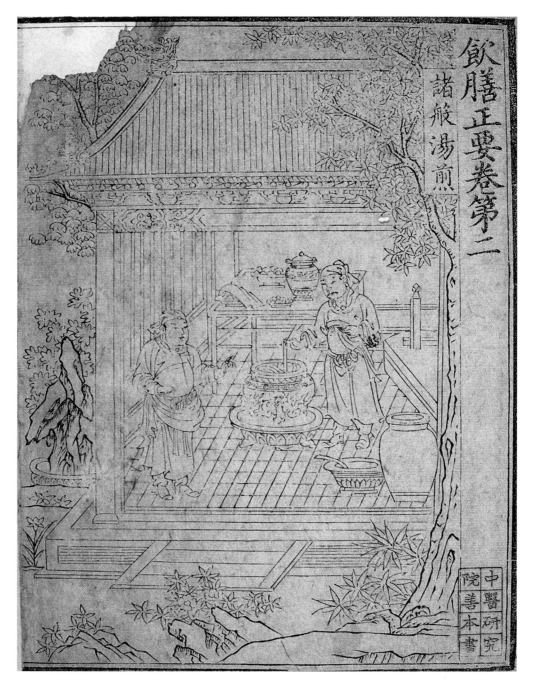

This woodcut shows the preparation of *Sihe tang* (Four Harmony Broth), which traditional Chinese medicine uses to help ease stomach problems.

FOOD ENERGY AND NUTRIENTS

Food energy is measured in calories, a word you probably recognize from the labels of food packages. A nutritional label lists how much energy is in a serving of food. It tells how much energy is provided by fat, carbohydrates, or protein. It also lists the content of certain nutrients, such as iron, calcium, and vitamins A and C. Other necessary nutrients not mentioned on nutrition labels include the B vitamins (thiamin, riboflavin, niacin, biotin, folic acid), vitamin D, vitamin E, magnesium, zinc, potassium, phosphorus, and selenium.

Teenagers have high calorie and nutrient needs because they are growing and developing rapidly. Moderately active 15-year-olds need between 2,000 and 2,400 calories per day. They also need 1,300 milligrams of calcium and between 11 and 15 milligrams of iron per day. A healthy diet is rich in foods that provide plenty of nutrients along with enough calories.

People who don't get enough to eat suffer from malnourishment, a lack of sufficient calories or nutrients. Even overweight and obese people can become malnourished if the foods they eat don't contain enough nutrients. Malnutrition can cause exhaustion, illnesses of various types, and, in children and adolescents, a failure to grow and develop.

"loss, absence, suppression, or scanty formation" of fecal matter. Some of the other symptoms described in millennia-old medical texts include abdominal pains, excess gas, and difficulty eating. But ancient physicians around the world had theories of disease that led them to attribute digestive problems—

along with most human illness—to imbalances in the diet and in the bodily "humors." Humors was their term for fluids or forces that were thought to control a person's health and personality.

In 16th-century Italy, physicians and scholars began studying the internal workings of the human body. They, and the scientists who followed them, have given us a much deeper understanding of how the digestive system works, the ways in which it can malfunction, and possible treatments that might help and heal.

A stone carving of an ancient Greek physician with his hand on a patient's abdomen.

"MANY VERY LITTLE LIVING ANIMALCULES"

Antonie van Leeuwenhoek

In 1683 a Dutch scientist named Antonie van Leeuwenhoek used a homemade microscope to examine samples he had taken from the inside of the mouths of two men on the street who said they had never cleaned their teeth. In the samples he found "an unbelievably great company of living animalcules, a-swimming more nimbly than any I had ever seen up to this time." These "animalcules" were what we now know as bacteria. It was the first proof we had that human bodies are home to microbes: bacteria, fungi, other single-celled life forms, and viruses.

Since then, scientists have discovered that our bodies are teeming with microbes. Communities of microbes live on our skin, in our mouths, and especially in our guts. Human intestines are home to some of the densest concentrations of microbial communities ever measured! These microbes affect the body in ways we are just beginning to investigate: some good, some bad, and some . . . well, it's complicated.

Collectively, the communities of human-dwelling microbes are known as the microbiota, or the microbiome. When scientists developed the tools for sequencing the human genome, they also discovered that a huge majority of the DNA we carry around isn't human at all, but that of the microbes that live inside us. Each person has a unique microbiota, which may help determine who we are just as much as our own DNA does.

Text-Dependent Questions

1. How do animals get the energy needed to support life?
2. What does a body need to do with food in order to make use of the energy and nutrients that food contains?
3. Name the organs of the digestive system in order. Explain how each of these organs contributes to the digestive process.

Research Project

A person eats a slice of pizza. Using the resources from the website of the National Institute of Diabetes and Digestive and Kidney Diseases (www.niddk.nih.gov/health-information/health-topics/Anatomy/your-digestive-system/Pages/anatomy.aspx), write the story of what happens to that slice of pizza as it travels through every stage of the digestive system. Are certain organs better at breaking down the carbohydrates in the pizza crust? What about the cheese?

WORDS TO UNDERSTAND

autoimmune: disease caused by immune cells attacking the body's own tissue.

chronic: going on for a long time; chronic diseases generally have no cure.

enzyme: a complex molecule produced by the body to cause or quicken biochemical reactions; digestive enzymes break down food molecules so that the small intestine can absorb nutrients.

gastroenterologist: a doctor specializing in diseases and disorders of the GI tract.

inflammation: redness, swelling, and tenderness in a part of the body in response to infection or injury.

intolerance: an inability to ingest a food without suffering negative effects.

motility: bodily tissues' ability to move, like the intestines' ability to perform peristalsis.

perforations: holes that penetrate through the walls or membranes of an organ or structure of the body.

syndrome: a set of symptoms or conditions that usually occur together, generally but not necessarily associated with a disease.

ulcers: a break or sore in skin or tissue where cells disintegrate and die. Infections may occur at the site of an ulcer.

CHAPTER TWO

Types of Digestive Disease

f you are one of the estimated 80,000 American kids with an inflammatory bowel disease, you have probably suffered stomach pains and an urgent need to poop, often at what feels like the worst possible time—in class, while playing sports, at a store or restaurant, or even while stuck in the car. Maybe you've wondered how inflammation can make you so miserable. What is inflammation, anyway?

Inflammation is the body's normal response to irritation, infection, or injury. It occurs when the body's immune system detects a problem that requires response and repair. Over the short term, inflammation helps the body to heal itself. But over a longer period of time, inflammation hurts the body. An **autoimmune** disease occurs when the reactions of the body's immune system cause long-term inflammation. Inflamed tissue becomes hot, red, swollen, and painful. It's prone to bleeding and injury. **Ulcers**, a type of open sore, can develop and become infected. In the digestive system, **chronic** inflammation causes serious damage.

Facts about IBD

In 1932, three doctors at Mt. Sinai Hospital in New York City published a paper about something they called "regional ileitis." They described patients with severe, chronic inflammation in the last section of the small intestine. The authors of this breakthrough paper were listed in alphabetical order: Crohn, Ginzburg, and Oppenheimer. Soon **gastroenterologists**, medical specialists in digestive disease, were using the first name on the paper as a kind of shorthand to refer to chronic inflammation in the ileum. Thus "Crohn's disease" was born. At the time, this was thought to be a rare and highly unusual condition. But Crohn's disease and other similar diseases have become markedly more common since the early 20th century. They affect well over a million people in the United States alone—and the numbers continue to rise.

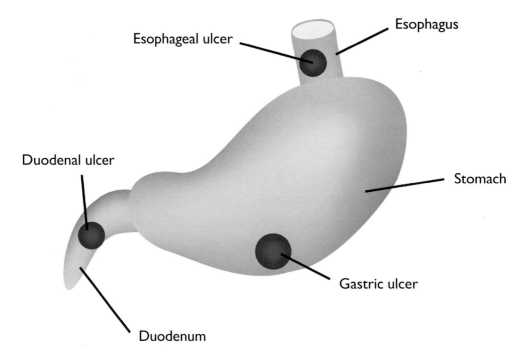

Ulcers can appear at various points in the digestive system.

Digestive disorders are specific to each person; people have to learn what foods they can digest and what they need to avoid. But many people with digestive issues avoid cow's milk and substitute other types, such as almond milk.

MALNUTRITION AND IBD

A person with almost any kind of digestive disease or disorder may have discomfort or difficulty eating and using the bathroom. That in itself can make it hard to get enough nutrients through a healthy, balanced diet. But when Crohn's disease causes inflammation in the small intestine, malnutrition becomes a serious concern. When the walls of the small intestine are damaged by inflammation, energy and nutrients may not be successfully absorbed into the bloodstream and lymphatic system for use around the body. People experiencing a severe flare-up of Crohn's disease may require supplements of vitamins and other nutrients until the intestinal walls can heal.

Because nutrients are generally absorbed by the small intestine before they can reach the colon, people with ulcerative colitis are less likely to suffer from malnutrition than people with Crohn's. But they are just as likely to struggle with anemia, weight loss, and exhaustion, as well as abdominal pain and other symptoms that can make them reluctant to eat. It can be hard to stay well nourished under these circumstances, but it is always important to try.

Crohn's disease is one of a category of chronic autoimmune illnesses known as inflammatory bowel disease (IBD). The other major IBD is called "ulcerative colitis." Ulcerative colitis is somewhat more common in the population as a whole, afflicting some 900,000 people in the United States. But Crohn's is more common among children and teens. Of the approximately 780,000 people in the United States with Crohn's disease, 20 to 30 percent were diagnosed before their 20th birthday. Both Crohn's and colitis cause chronic inflammation in the GI tract. They create swelling, ulcers, and other serious complications that can damage organs.

How Do You Get an IBD?

If you come down with the flu, doctors know how you got it: you came into contact with a virus that causes flu. But for Crohn's disease and ulcerative colitis, it's not so simple. No one knows exactly what causes IBD. We do know that IBDs are not infectious—you can't catch them from anyone else or give them to anyone else. We also know that you can't get an IBD from eating the wrong thing.

But then how do you get an IBD? While we don't know for sure, scientists have identified certain risk factors—things that make it more or less likely that any given person develops any given disease. These risk factors include the following:

EDUCATIONAL VIDEO

Scan the QR code for a video about a young person with IBD.

- **Genetics.** IBD tends to run in families. Thanks to new methods of DNA sequencing, scientists have found more than 100 genetic mutations associated with IBD. But many people with one or more of these mutations never get an IBD. Scientists think genetic mutations affect a person's susceptibility to other factors involved in IBD.

- **The immune system.** Some people's immune systems are more likely to overreact to real or perceived threats, damaging the body's own tissues. These people are more likely to develop autoimmune diseases like IBD.

- **Environmental triggers.** This refers not only to the literal environment but to any conditions people experience in daily life. Strong evidence suggests that smoking is an environmental trigger for Crohn's. The evidence for other triggers is not as strong. Scientists are investigating whether antibiotics or other drugs, infectious disease, foodborne illness, diet, hygiene, stress, and socioeconomic status might play a role in the development of IBD.

- **The microbiome.** The communities of microbes living in the intestines of people with IBD show significant differences from those of people without IBD. But scientists do not yet know whether these differences are a cause of disease or a symptom of it.

Unfortunately, knowing some of the risk factors for IBD doesn't tell us how to prevent IBD. But it does give us some promising avenues for further research. This research may someday lead to a real understanding of the causes of IBD. Research has already taught us a lot about how IBD affects the digestive system.

Inflammation inside the GI Tract

Crohn's disease can occur in any part of the GI tract, from the mouth to the anus. But it is most likely to cause inflammation at the end of the small

Normal

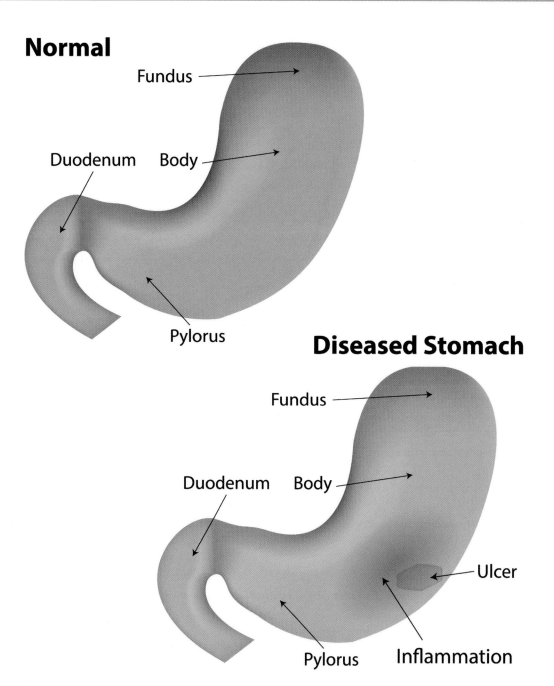

Fundus

Duodenum   Body

Pylorus

Diseased Stomach

Fundus

Duodenum   Body

Ulcer

Pylorus   Inflammation

Crohn's disease can strike anywhere along the digestive tract. This diagram compares a healthy stomach and a stomach with Crohn's.

intestine, the ileum. If the inflammation lasts for a long time, ulcers can form, and they may eat all the way through the intestinal wall. Digestive and fecal matter can leak through these holes in the GI tract. They can leak from one part of the GI tract to another, out of the GI tract to elsewhere in the body, or even outside the body through the skin.

These tunneling ulcers are called fistulas. They are one of the most distressing complications of Crohn's disease. Other complications include scarring, swelling, and thickening of the intestinal walls. These can block the GI tract such that it can be difficult or even impossible for digestive matter to pass through. All of these complications can be very painful, and in some cases they can be life-threatening. Surgery is sometimes required to address them.

In ulcerative colitis, inflammation occurs only in the large intestine (the colon and the rectum). It spreads continuously, rather than in patches. Ulcers form in the thin, innermost layer of the colon wall, the mucosa. Because the ulcers do not penetrate the wall of the colon, fistulas do not generally occur with ulcerative colitis. But **perforations** can occur due to infection or injury. In very severe cases of ulcerative colitis, the entire colon may become inflamed and swollen. This may cause peristalsis to fail, preventing fecal matter from moving to the anus and out of the body. This condition, called *toxic megacolon*, is rare, but requires immediate medical treatment.

In both Crohn's disease and ulcerative colitis, inflamed walls of the GI tract may bleed when digestive or fecal matter passes through. Blood in the stool and bloody diarrhea are characteristic symptoms of IBD. The loss of blood can cause anemia, a condition caused by having too few red blood cells; anemia causes exhaustion and other symptoms. Abdominal pain is another common symptom of IBD.

Beyond the GI Tract

Inflammatory bowel disease is associated with certain problems beyond the digestive system. People with IBD are more likely to experience inflammation of the eyes (called uveitis or iritis depending on which part of the eyes are affected). Skin rashes, ulcers, and psoriasis are also more common in people with IBD. Doctors don't know exactly why these other disorders tend to go hand-in-hand with IBD. In some cases, problems like psoriasis may be side effects of IBD treatment, while in other cases they seem to appear on their own.

As many as one-quarter of people with IBD also suffer from a condition called arthritis. Arthritis is an inflammation of the joints that connect our

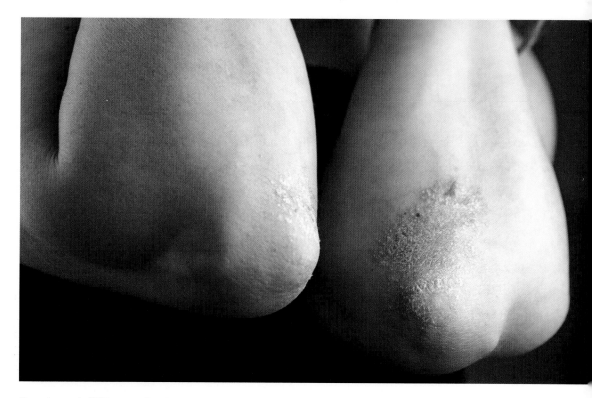

People with IBD may also have to deal with an itchy skin condition called psoriasis.

bones to each other—people often experience arthritis in their knees, elbows, and hands. There are a few different types of arthritis that can affect people with IBD. Peripheral arthritis affects the arms and legs, and is generally temporary; it improves when other IBD symptoms improve. More serious is axial arthritis, also known as spondylitis, which inflames and stiffens the spine. Axial arthritis may not respond to treatment of the underlying IBD.

A small group of people with IBD (about 2 to 3 percent) develop ankylosing spondylitis, a severe form of arthritis that stiffens the spine and causes inflammation in the eyes, lungs, and heart valves. Some of the newer drug treatments for IBD also treat ankylosing spondylitis. Researchers hope that unlocking more of the secrets of the body's immune system will point the way to even more effective treatments for IBD and its complications.

Other Digestive Disorders

Celiac Disease. Gluten is a protein found in grains such as wheat, rye, and barley. It's present in many common foods. Bread, pizza, burritos, pretzels, cake, cookies, muffins—all of these contain gluten unless they are specifically labeled "gluten-free."

Worldwide, up to 1 percent of the population has a condition called celiac disease. For these people, gluten is a big problem. In celiac disease, the body has an immune reaction to gluten in the small intestine, causing inflammation. This inflammation can cause serious damage to the small intestine over time. People with celiac disease can become malnourished when intestinal damage limits their ability to absorb nutrients. They may also suffer digestive symptoms and other complaints caused by an overactive immune system.

For most people with celiac disease, going on a strict gluten-free diet allows the small intestine to heal. They do not need to take any medications, but they

People with celiac disease have to be extremely careful to avoid foods with gluten.

do need to continue avoiding gluten their entire lives. It can be challenging to maintain such a diet.

Doctors do not yet understand what causes celiac disease. It runs in families, so genetic susceptibility is clearly a factor. But the microbiota might offer valuable clues as to why some people develop celiac disease and others don't.

Irritable Bowel Syndrome. Irritable bowel **syndrome**, or IBS, sounds a lot like IBD. It can have similar symptoms, like stomach pains, cramps, and diarrhea

THE STORY OF GLUTEN AND FRUCTANS

For a while, anyone with digestive problems might have gotten advice from well-meaning friends and family to go "gluten-free." Many people tried avoiding foods containing gluten. Some of them reported feeling better. But doctors and nutritionists argued that there's little scientific evidence to support cutting out gluten for better health —except for people with celiac disease. But some people who don't have celiac disease also reported feeling better after giving up gluten. Why?

The answer might lie not in gluten, but in the carbohydrates that go along with gluten. Wheat contains a lot of a carbohydrate called fructan. Fructans are poorly absorbed by the small intestine. What isn't absorbed gets moved on to the large intestine, where the microbes in the gut ferment it. Fermentation breaks substances down, but it creates a lot of gas in the process. This can cause pain, discomfort, bloating, and other complaints. A diet lower in fermentable carbohydrates can reduce gas. It may even change the microbiota in the gut. But it can also be difficult and expensive to stay well-nourished while avoiding foods with fermentable carbohydrates. The evidence has not yet proved that this kind of diet can help people with IBD.

(or constipation). But when doctors look at images of the digestive tract of someone with IBS, they see no sign of tissue damage or inflammation. Nothing looks wrong.

IBS is a functional gastrointestinal disorder affecting intestinal **motility**. That means the GI tract behaves abnormally when it's moving digestive matter along. Because IBS causes no physical damage, it poses no known health risk. But it is still no fun to live with.

IBS is extremely common. It is chronic, but symptoms can vary over time. People who have it are more likely to suffer from indigestion, anxiety, and depression. They may also suffer from gastroesophageal reflux disease, or GERD (also known as acid reflux), a condition in which the contents of the stomach move backwards up the esophagus.

Doctors do not know what causes IBS. Current research suggests that therapies for managing stress, anxiety, and emotional difficulties can help control IBS. But scientists are also exploring whether other factors may be involved. Many of these factors are common to other digestive disorders, including genetics, changes in the microbiota, and difficulties absorbing certain nutrients. Scientists think there may be a connection between IBS and unusual sensitivity or malfunctions in the signals sent between the gut and the brain.

Lactose Intolerance. Human beings are born with the ability to digest lactose, a sugar found in milk. The small intestine produces an **enzyme** called lactase, which breaks complex lactose molecules into two simple sugar molecules, glucose and galactose. The lactase enzyme allows babies to grow and thrive on mother's milk. For most of human history, mother's milk was the only dairy product anyone had. Once a young child was weaned, the body had no further need for the lactase enzyme, and stopped producing it.

Eventually, some cultures began farming animals like cows and water buffaloes for their milk. In modern times, dairy foods such as milk, cheese, and ice cream are easy to come by the world over. But many people still lose the ability to digest lactose as they get older. This is called lactose **intolerance**. This condition can also develop as a result of illness or injury to the tissues of the small intestine.

If you are lactose intolerant and you eat dairy products, the lactose in your food passes undigested from your small intestine to your colon. In your large intestine, bacteria enthusiastically consume that lactose. That may cause you to develop gas, bloating, diarrhea, and discomfort. Most people with lactose intolerance can handle small amounts of dairy in their diet without suffering discomfort. If you can't, you might regret having a slice of cheesy pizza or an ice cream cone. But you're not damaging your body by eating them.

Fortunately for people with lactose intolerance, there are specialized dairy-based products that are lactose free.

Text-Dependent Questions

1. What is inflammation? What happens to inflamed tissues?
2. What are some of the differences between Crohn's disease and ulcerative colitis? What are some similarities?
3. List three complications of IBD that can occur somewhere in the body besides the digestive system.

Research Project

The website of the Crohn's & Colitis Foundation of America includes a "GI Tract Guide," which can be found at http://gitract.ccfa.org. Use this interactive tool to explore the symptoms and complications caused by IBD. How many different parts of the body can be affected by IBD? Which areas of the GI tract are most likely to be affected by IBD? Which areas of the GI tract are most likely to have only mild symptoms, or none at all? What are some of the differences between the complications of Crohn's disease and those of ulcerative colitis? What are some similarities?

WORDS TO UNDERSTAND

biologic therapies: medications made from lab-grown human antibodies that selectively target particular proteins that cause inflammation; also called biologics.

corticosteroids: a type of hormone produced by the body's adrenal cortex; also made synthetically in a lab for use as a medication to treat inflammation.

endoscopy: an imaging procedure in which a doctor threads a long, flexible tube bearing a camera into the GI tract; called a colonoscopy when the tube is inserted through the anus into the colon.

immunomodulators: drugs that act broadly on the immune system to reduce or stimulate its activity; also called immunologics.

intravenously: put directly into veins using a needle.

prognosis: the forecast for the course of a disease that predicts whether a person with the disease will get sicker, recover, or stay the same.

remission: an improvement in or disappearance of someone's symptoms of disease; unlike a cure, remission is usually temporary.

CHAPTER THREE

Diagnosis and Treatment of IBD

When Dr. Burrill B. Crohn was in medical school in the early 20th century, a professor told him not to bother learning about the small intestine. It got no diseases, said the professor, "except, perhaps, tuberculosis." Dr. Crohn himself went on to prove his professor wrong. He and other scientists proved that Crohn's disease not only exists, but also that it has nothing to do with tuberculosis.

The discoveries of Crohn and his fellow scientists were hardly the last word, however. Our understanding of IBD continues to change, and new developments are reported in scientific journals every month. Together, they may soon revolutionize treatments for IBD. They are also shedding light on other digestive diseases and disorders. It can be scary to be diagnosed with a chronic disease, but the future has never been brighter for people with digestive diseases.

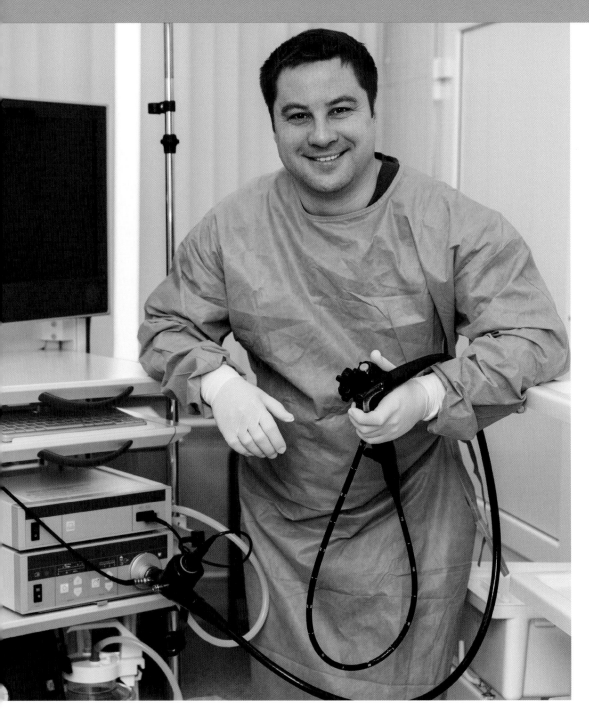

An endoscope is a special type of diagnostic tool that allows doctors to see what is going on inside a person's digestive system.

From Diagnosis to Treatment

To confirm your diagnosis, your doctor may have conducted an **endoscopy** or colonoscopy. In this procedure, a doctor inserts a very long, flexible tube called an endoscope into the GI tract, either through the mouth or the anus. The tube contains a tiny camera, allowing the doctor to actually see whether the walls of your GI tract are inflamed. A person is sedated with anesthesia during an endoscopy. The procedure does not hurt. Once you, your family, and your doctors have decided on a treatment plan, you may have follow-up endoscopies every so often to check on how well your medications are controlling inflammation.

EDUCATIONAL VIDEO

Scan this QR code for a video where kids discuss their IBD.

Your doctor might prescribe one or more medications for you. Drugs called **corticosteroids** work quickly and are often prescribed when the goal is to end a flare-up. Corticosteroids have been in use for many decades. They can have troubling side effects, however, especially when used for a long time. While newer corticosteroids such as budesonide have far fewer side effects than older drugs, your doctor is likely to recommend another type of drug for long-term use.

Two newer classes of drugs are used to treat IBD. **Immunomodulators** make the immune system less active. **Biologic therapies** use human antibodies grown in a laboratory to reduce the activity of specific parts of the immune system. By quieting the immune system, these drugs reduce inflammation in the GI tract. In some cases, they can eliminate all signs of inflammation.

FECAL TRANSPLANTS

There are many ways to change the microbes that live in your gut. What you eat affects your population of microbes. Ordinary foods can encourage or discourage certain types of microbes. Probiotics are foods specially manufactured to contain specific helpful organisms. Many kinds of yogurt contain probiotics.

Doctors have had some success changing a person's microbiota via the other end of the GI tract. In a fecal transplant, a doctor takes poop from a healthy person and puts it inside a sick person via the anus. This sounds gross, but it's proved to be the most effective treatment for certain life-threatening infections of the colon. Researchers are still studying whether fecal transplants can play a role in treating IBD.

When inflammation is reduced or eliminated, people with IBD feel much better. They have fewer symptoms, or even none at all. They are also much less likely to develop complications. Their disease is said to be in **remission**. Remission is the goal of treatment for IBD. Scientists keep searching for even more effective ways to put IBD into remission.

It may take a while to find a medication—or a combination of medications—that works best for you. You may take pills one or more times a day. Some IBD drugs are delivered every few weeks via an injection that you can get at home. Other drugs may be administered **intravenously** by a trained nurse at a special medical clinic called an infusion center.

Besides regular visits to check in with your doctor, you might have an endoscopy, a colonoscopy, an MRI, a barium X-ray, or another imaging test. You may also have occasional blood tests to check for certain markers of inflammation. In periods of remission, your doctors' appointments and your medications may be the only reminders you have of IBD.

Uniquely You

Each person with IBD is unique. Scientists now believe that each case of Crohn's disease or ulcerative colitis may result from a unique combination of different factors. One person may have many genetic susceptibilities to IBD, and thus may develop disease after exposure to only a few environmental triggers. Another person may only have one or two genetic risk factors, and

It can take some time for your health-care providers to figure out the best treatment.

Each case of IBD is slightly different and may need to be addressed differently.

thus develop disease only after experiencing many different environmental triggers. Doctors think the future of IBD treatment lies in addressing the factors that led to each individual's unique disease.

Some of the most interesting research today focuses on the microbiome. Researchers are only just beginning to map the diversity of the organisms that live in the human gut. But they are hoping to discover whether certain types of microbes are associated with IBD. They want to know if changing the microbes that live in your GI tract can also change the **prognosis** for people with IBD. Scientists are looking at several different ways to affect the microbes that live in the gut.

Doctors today are very hopeful that we will soon be able to prevent some people with certain risk factors from ever getting an IBD. They think that the treatments we have now will be improved so that people who do have IBD will live healthier and easier lives. And, best of all, they think that eventually there will be a cure for at least some types of IBD.

Text-Dependent Questions

1. List some ways that doctors treat IBD. What kinds of medications are used?
2. What are the benefits of reducing or eliminating inflammation?
3. What is the goal of treatment for IBD?

Research Project

The website of the Crohn's & Colitis Foundation maintains a page outlining the types of medications used to treat IBD. It can be found at www.ccfa.org/resources/types-of-medications.html. Click on the links to learn more about the five types of medications currently recommended for use against IBD, or watch the video on the right side of the page. Do these medications have something in common? What system of the body do they target?

WORDS TO UNDERSTAND

accommodation: an arrangement or adjustment to a new situation; for example, schools make accommodations to help students cope with illness.

fiber: the parts of food that digestive enzymes cannot break down.

flare-up: in IBD, a sudden outburst of the symptoms of disease.

ostomy: a type of surgery that creates an opening in the body for the disposal of bodily wastes, such as stool or urine; an ileostomy creates an opening in the ileum of the small intestine.

relapse: when the symptoms of a disease get worse after a period of being better.

stoma: an opening in a hollow organ, like the intestines, connected to a hole surgically cut in the surface of the body.

stricture: a narrowing of a hollow organ that prevents it from performing its function.

CHAPTER FOUR

Living with Active IBD

Stomach pain. Frequent diarrhea, which may cause embarrassing accidents. Weight loss. Exhaustion. If you or someone you love has been diagnosed with an inflammatory bowel disease, these symptoms are probably familiar. For people with active Crohn's disease or ulcerative colitis, daily life can sometimes be a struggle.

Inflammatory bowel disease tends to cycle through quieter periods and active stages, called **flare-ups**. If you are diagnosed with an IBD while experiencing the symptoms of a flare-up, your doctor's first priority will be to end the flare-up so that you can return to normal daily life. The next priority will be maintaining your remission. The goal is to heal the inflammation in your GI tract, making it less likely that you'll experience a **relapse**. Medication and diet are two key tools to support these goals.

Because every person with IBD is unique, different people might have different dietary requirements. Doctors generally recommend that people with IBD avoid large nuts, seeds, and popcorn, because they are hard for the stomach to break down and can get stuck in the digestive tract. They

Some people with IBD have a lot of trouble with tomatoes; for other people, it could be fried foods or dairy that cause the worst problems.

may also suggest avoiding foods high in **fiber**. But other recommendations will vary depending on the person. For example, some people may have more stomach pain or diarrhea after eating tomatoes. Another person might have no problem with tomatoes, but feel terrible after eating fried foods like potato chips or French fries. Other people might need to

EDUCATIONAL VIDEO

Scan this code for a video about living with IBD.

avoid dairy products during a flare-up. You, your family, and your doctors will work together to determine what foods you should avoid during flare-ups or to prevent flare-ups.

In the Bag: Surgery and IBD

In very severe cases, Crohn's disease or ulcerative colitis may not respond to medications. Doctors may recommend surgery to remove the diseased tissue in the GI tract and provide relief from symptoms. For people with Crohn's disease, surgery is usually because of a health-threatening emergency, like a **stricture** or blockage in the GI tract. But some people with ulcerative colitis decide to have their colon and rectums surgically removed in a procedure called a proctocolectomy. Surgeons removing the large intestine will then perform an ileostomy, connecting the end of the small intestine to a **stoma**, a small opening cut through the belly. An external plastic bag called an **ostomy** bag is attached to the skin around the stoma. This bag holds fecal matter as it empties from the small intestine.

HAIL TO THE CHIEF

President Dwight D. Eisenhower

President John F. Kennedy

There's no tougher or more demanding job than being president of the United States. But two people have managed that job while also managing IBD.

President Dwight D. Eisenhower was a five-star general and one of the most decorated and respected heroes of World War II. He also had Crohn's disease. The American public only learned of it when President Eisenhower had emergency surgery in 1956 for a bowel obstruction. At the time, not much was known about Crohn's disease. Reporters called Dr. Crohn himself for answers about the president's illness.

President John F. Kennedy had many health issues throughout his life. He is believed to have suffered from ulcerative colitis, starting as a teenager. The steroids he took for his colitis may have been part of the reason he developed severe back problems and a hormonal disorder called Addison's disease. He lived much of his life battling terrible pain, but never let it stop him.

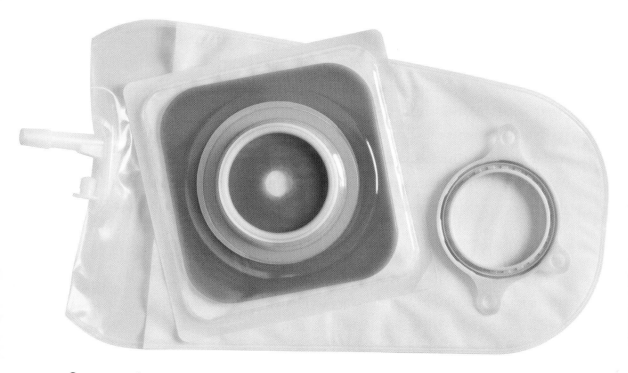

Ostomy equipment.

The ostomy bag may only be temporary. After the first surgery has healed, surgeons will operate again to create an small internal pouch at the end of the small intestine, and connect that to the anus. This allows people to pass stool normally again.

In other cases, the ostomy bag is permanent. Since ulcerative colitis only occurs in the colon and rectum, people who have these organs removed are effectively cured of ulcerative colitis. Some people feel that the trade-off is worth it.

Coping with Flare-Ups

While the goal of IBD treatment is to achieve remission, you may sometimes find yourself coping with a flare-up. A relapse can occur for many reasons, and those reasons can vary from person to person. Some people experience flare-ups when they are very stressed by things going on at school or at home. Some people relapse if they reduce or change their medications. Other people relapse when the medications they are on become less effective for them.

No matter what causes it, a relapse can make daily life a lot more difficult. You may need to use the bathroom so urgently that you don't have time to wait. You may find that stomach pain or exhaustion makes it difficult to concentrate in school. You may struggle with sports or other extracurricular activities. You may worry about what your friends will think if they find out about your IBD. You may feel like you're the only person going through something like this. But you're definitely not alone. Thousands and thousands of other kids have been through the same thing. And there are some steps you and your family can take to make your life a little easier during a flare-up.

At school, your administrators, teachers, and nurses or counselors should be aware of your IBD. They may suggest that your family and your doctors prepare a list of **accommodations** that will help you get through the school day. This is called a 504 plan. Many kids with IBD find it helpful to have blanket permission

ALIEN . . . OR IBD?

In the classic 1979 sci-fi horror film *Alien*, a spaceship crew is terrorized by an alien life form that stalks them from various hiding places on the ship. The movie's most memorable scene terrified generations of movie fans. A crew member begins writhing in pain—and then the alien erupts from *inside* his torso.

What was the inspiration for this famous exploding alien? Screenwriter Dan O'Bannon said he got the idea from his experiences with Crohn's disease.

Sometimes it's helpful to keep supplies in your locker just in case of emergency.

OLYMPIC MEDALS

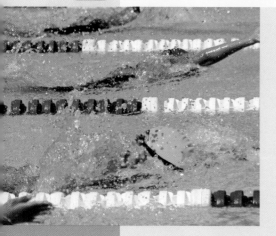

The swimmer Kathleen Baker was 12 years old when she set her first two national records for her age group. That was also the year she first began to suffer the symptoms of what was eventually diagnosed as Crohn's disease. She remembers eighth grade as a "nightmare" of doctors' visits, stomach pain, illness, and weight loss. In a 2016 interview with the *New York Times*, she said, "I love swimming more than anything in the entire world, and I thought my swimming career was over."

Despite the concerns of her parents, doctors, and coaches, she fought to be allowed to continue to train during flare-ups. Together they were able to modify her training regimen so she could keep swimming and competing despite her disease. Sometimes she struggled, but she remained determined. Finally, she and her doctors found a medication that put her into remission.

Through it all, Baker managed to become a champion. She won four gold medals at the 2013 world junior championship, and a silver the following year at senior nationals. At 19 she made the U.S. Olympic team to compete at the 2016 Summer Olympics in Brazil. Baker then won a silver medal in the women's 100-meter backstroke, and a gold medal in the women's 4x100-meter medley relay. Her medals are a tremendous victory for anyone who has ever been afraid of losing their dreams to IBD.

to use the bathroom whenever necessary. If you are embarrassed to use the bathroom in front of other people, find out if your school has a more private bathroom that you could use, perhaps near the nurse's office.

You may also want to assemble a plastic baggie that you could keep in your backpack, locker, or the nurse's office. You might include a change of clothes, wipes or toilet paper, and any other supplies you might need if you have an accident. If you have to miss school because of doctors' appointments, illness, or hospitalizations, it helps to have a plan on file spelling out how you and the school will handle your absences.

You can decide to tell certain friends about your Crohn's or to keep it private. It's up to you.

It's up to you to decide how much to tell your friends and classmates about your IBD. You may appreciate having the support of your friends. You may prefer to maintain your privacy. There is no right or wrong answer—only what is comfortable for you.

If you do talk to your friends, they may have questions about whether they can catch IBD from you. They can't. Crohn's disease and ulcerative colitis aren't infectious. They may also want to know if you will die from IBD. You won't. You will have periods of remission, and you may struggle sometimes with flare-ups. But your IBD won't stop you from leading a normal life.

 ## Text-Dependent Questions

1. Dietary recommendations for people with IBD vary from person to person. Why is this? Are there any foods that people with IBD generally avoid?
2. What is an ostomy? What is its purpose?
3. Why do some people with ulcerative colitis choose to have their rectums and colons surgically removed?

 ## Research Project

The Crohn's & Colitis Foundation of America produces a fact sheet to help students with IBD, their parents or guardians, and schools make a plan of accommodations. You can read through it here: www.ccfa. org/resources/new-school-accommodation.pdf. If you have IBD, you can print it out to share and discuss with your family. Does it include suggestions that are helpful to you? Write down your ideas for how your friends, family, and school can support you. If you don't have IBD, what are some things you could do to be supportive of a friend or classmate with the disease?

FURTHER READING

Staton, Hilarie. *Pete Learns All about Crohn's and Colitis.* New York: Crohn's & Colitis Foundation of America, 2010. http://www.ccfa.org/assets/pdfs/pete-learns-all-about-crohns.pdf.

———. *A Guide for Teens with IBD.* New York: Crohn's & Colitis Foundation of America, 2014. http://www.ccfa.org/assets/pdfs/teenguide.pdf.

Steinhart, A. Hillary. *Crohn's & Colitis: Understanding and Managing IBD.* Toronto: Robert Rose, 2012.

Tauseef, Ali. *Crohn's & Colitis for Dummies.* Mississaugua, ON: John Wiley & Sons Canada, 2013.

The Facts about Inflammatory Bowel Diseases. New York: Crohn's & Colitis Foundation of America, 2014. http://www.ccfa.org/assets/pdfs/ibdfactbook.pdf.

Warner, Andrew S., and Amy E. Barto. *100 Questions & Answers about Crohn's Disease and Ulcerative Colitis: A Lahey Clinic Guide.* Sudbury, MA: Jones and Bartlett, 2010.

Educational Videos

Chapter 1: Khan Academy. "The Digestive System." https://www.khanacademy.org/partner-content/crash-course1/partner-topic-crash-course-bio-ecology/crash-course-biology/v/crash-course-biology-127.

Chapter 2: Penn State Hershey IBD Center. "Hannah's Story." https://youtu.be/6u11NwSqq14.

Chapter 3: Crohn's & Colitis Foundation of America (CCFA). "If There Was a Pill That Made Your IBD Go Away, Would You Take It?" https://youtu.be/Yyrzp_fB6HE.

Chapter 4: Hank Green (hankschannel). "Living with a Chronic Disease." https://youtu.be/rr8wIiypS_g.

accommodation: an arrangement or adjustment to a new situation; for example, schools make accommodations to help students cope with illness.

anemia: an illness caused by a lack of red blood cells.

autoimmune: type of disorder where the body's immune system attacks the body's tissues instead of germs.

benign: not harmful.

biofeedback: a technique used to teach someone how to control some bodily functions.

capillaries: tiny blood vessels that carry blood from larger blood vessels to body tissues.

carcinogens: substances that can cause cancer to develop.

cerebellum: the back part of the brain; it controls movement.

cerebrum: the front part of the brain; it controls many higher-level thinking and functions.

cholesterol: a waxy substance associated with fats that coats the inside of blood vessels, causing cardiovascular disease.

cognitive: related to conscious mental activities, such as learning and thinking.

communicable: transferable from one person to another.

congenital: a condition or disorder that exists from birth.

correlation: a connection between different things that suggests they may have something to do with one another.

dominant: in genetics, a dominant trait is expressed in a child even when the trait is only inherited from one parent.

environmental factors: anything that affects how people live, develop, or grow. Climate, diet, and pollution are examples.

genes: units of hereditary information.

hemorrhage: bleeding from a broken blood vessel.

hormones: substances the body produces to instruct cells and tissues to perform certain actions.

inflammation: redness, swelling, and tenderness in a part of the body in response to infection or injury.

insulin: a hormone produced in the pancreas that controls cells' ability to absorb glucose.

lymphatic system: part of the human immune system; transports white blood cells around the body.

malignant: harmful; relating to tumors, likely to spread.

mutation: a change in the structure of a gene; some mutations are harmless, but others may cause disease.

neurological: relating to the nervous system (including the brain and spinal cord).

neurons: specialized cells found in the central nervous system (the brain and spinal cord).

occupational therapy: a type of therapy that teaches one how to accomplish tasks and activities in daily life.

oncology: the study of cancer.

orthopedic: dealing with deformities in bones or muscles.

prevalence: how common or uncommon a disease is in any given population.

prognosis: the forecast for the course of a disease that predicts whether a person with the disease will get sicker, recover, or stay the same.

progressive disease: a disease that generally gets worse as time goes on.

psychomotor: relating to movement or muscle activity resulting from mental activity.

recessive: in genetics, a recessive trait will only be expressed if a child inherits it from both parents.

remission: an improvement in or disappearance of someone's symptoms of disease; unlike a cure, remission is usually temporary.

resilience: the ability to bounce back from difficult situations.

seizure: an event caused by unusual brain activity resulting in physical or behavior changes.

syndrome: a condition with a set of associated symptoms.

ulcers: a break or sore in skin or tissue where cells disintegrate and die. Infections may occur at the site of an ulcer.

INDEX

Illlustrations are indicated by page numbers in *italic* type.

ABOUT THE ADVISOR

Heather Pelletier, Ph.D., is a pediatric staff psychologist at Rhode Island Hospital/Hasbro Children's Hospital with a joint appointment as a clinical assistant professor in the departments of Psychiatry and Human Behavior and Pediatrics at the Warren Alpert Medical School of Brown University. She is also the director of behavioral pain medicine in the division of Children's Integrative therapies, Pain management and Supportive care (CHIPS) in the department of Pediatrics at Hasbro Children's Hospital. Dr. Pelletier provides clinical services to children in various medical specialty clinics at Hasbro Children's Hospital, including the pediatric gastroenterology, nutrition, and liver disease clinics.

ABOUT THE AUTHOR

Rebecca Sherman writes about health care policy, public health issues, and parenting. She lives in Massachusetts with her family.

PHOTO CREDITS

Cover: istock/PeopleImages
iStock: 10 AndreyPopov; 12 joebelanger; 13 asiseeit; 14 ChrisGorgio; 25 Rocky89; 26 KatarzynaBialasiewicz ; 33 chameleonseye; 36 minoandriani ; 40 kot63; 43 XiXinXing; 48 hdagli; 51 Copestello; 54 LeeAnnWhite
Library of Congress: 50
Shutterstock: 24 Timonina; 29 joshya; 31 Hriana; 44 Iakov Filimonov; 53 Zimiri; 55 Monkey Business Images
Wellcome Images: 17; 19
Wikimedia: 20 Jan Verkolje; 50 White House Press Office